AUTO MILEAGE LOG AND EXPENSE RECORD

Copyright 2014

AUTO MILEAGE AND EXPENSE LOG

MONTH:________________

DATE	PLACE, PERSON OR TASK	START	STOP	MILES	TOLLS	MISC.

AUTO MILEAGE AND EXPENSE LOG

MONTH:________________

DATE	PLACE, PERSON OR TASK	START	STOP	MILES	TOLLS	MISC.

MONTH:________________

AUTO MILEAGE AND EXPENSE LOG

MONTH:_______________

DATE	PLACE, PERSON OR TASK	START	STOP	MILES	TOLLS	MISC.

AUTO MILEAGE AND EXPENSE LOG

MONTH:____________________

DATE	PLACE, PERSON OR TASK	START	STOP	MILES	TOLLS	MISC.

AUTO MILEAGE AND EXPENSE LOG

MONTH: _______________

DATE	PLACE, PERSON OR TASK	START	STOP	MILES	TOLLS	MISC.

MONTH:

AUTO MILEAGE AND EXPENSE LOG

MONTH:_______________

DATE	PLACE, PERSON OR TASK	START	STOP	MILES	TOLLS	MISC.

AUTO MILEAGE AND EXPENSE LOG

MONTH:________________

DATE	PLACE, PERSON OR TASK	START	STOP	MILES	TOLLS	MISC.

AUTO MILEAGE AND EXPENSE LOG

MONTH:_________________

DATE	PLACE, PERSON OR TASK	START	STOP	MILES	TOLLS	MISC.

AUTO MILEAGE AND EXPENSE LOG

MONTH: _______________

DATE	PLACE, PERSON OR TASK	START	STOP	MILES	TOLLS	MISC.

AUTO MILEAGE AND EXPENSE LOG

MONTH:________________

DATE	PLACE, PERSON OR TASK	START	STOP	MILES	TOLLS	MISC.

AUTO MILEAGE AND EXPENSE LOG

MONTH:_________________

DATE	PLACE, PERSON OR TASK	START	STOP	MILES	TOLLS	MISC.

AUTO MILEAGE AND EXPENSE LOG

MONTH:________________

DATE	PLACE, PERSON OR TASK	START	STOP	MILES	TOLLS	MISC.

AUTO MILEAGE AND EXPENSE LOG

MONTH: _______________

DATE	PLACE, PERSON OR TASK	START	STOP	MILES	TOLLS	MISC.

AUTO MILEAGE AND EXPENSE LOG

MONTH:________________

DATE	PLACE, PERSON OR TASK	START	STOP	MILES	TOLLS	MISC.

AUTO MILEAGE AND EXPENSE LOG

MONTH: _______________

DATE	PLACE, PERSON OR TASK	START	STOP	MILES	TOLLS	MISC.

AUTO MILEAGE AND EXPENSE LOG

MONTH:_________________

DATE	PLACE, PERSON OR TASK	START	STOP	MILES	TOLLS	MISC.

AUTO MILEAGE AND EXPENSE LOG

MONTH:________________

DATE	PLACE, PERSON OR TASK	START	STOP	MILES	TOLLS	MISC.

MONTH:________________

AUTO MILEAGE AND EXPENSE LOG

MONTH: _______________

DATE	PLACE, PERSON OR TASK	START	STOP	MILES	TOLLS	MISC.

AUTO MILEAGE AND EXPENSE LOG

MONTH: ________________

DATE	PLACE, PERSON OR TASK	START	STOP	MILES	TOLLS	MISC.

AUTO MILEAGE AND EXPENSE LOG

MONTH: _______________

DATE	PLACE, PERSON OR TASK	START	STOP	MILES	TOLLS	MISC.

AUTO MILEAGE AND EXPENSE LOG

MONTH:_________________

DATE	PLACE, PERSON OR TASK	START	STOP	MILES	TOLLS	MISC.

MONTH:

AUTO MILEAGE AND EXPENSE LOG

MONTH:_______________

DATE	PLACE, PERSON OR TASK	START	STOP	MILES	TOLLS	MISC.

AUTO MILEAGE AND EXPENSE LOG

MONTH:________________

DATE	PLACE, PERSON OR TASK	START	STOP	MILES	TOLLS	MISC.

MONTH:

AUTO MILEAGE AND EXPENSE LOG

MONTH:_______________

DATE	PLACE, PERSON OR TASK	START	STOP	MILES	TOLLS	MISC.

AUTO MILEAGE AND EXPENSE LOG

MONTH:________________

DATE	PLACE, PERSON OR TASK	START	STOP	MILES	TOLLS	MISC.

MONTH:

AUTO MILEAGE AND EXPENSE LOG

MONTH:_________________

DATE	PLACE, PERSON OR TASK	START	STOP	MILES	TOLLS	MISC.

AUTO MILEAGE AND EXPENSE LOG

MONTH: ______________

DATE	PLACE, PERSON OR TASK	START	STOP	MILES	TOLLS	MISC.

MONTH: ______________

AUTO MILEAGE AND EXPENSE LOG

MONTH: _______________

DATE	PLACE, PERSON OR TASK	START	STOP	MILES	TOLLS	MISC.

AUTO MILEAGE AND EXPENSE LOG

MONTH:________________

DATE	PLACE, PERSON OR TASK	START	STOP	MILES	TOLLS	MISC.

MONTH:

AUTO MILEAGE AND EXPENSE LOG

MONTH:_________________

DATE	PLACE, PERSON OR TASK	START	STOP	MILES	TOLLS	MISC.

AUTO MILEAGE AND EXPENSE LOG

MONTH: _______________

DATE	PLACE, PERSON OR TASK	START	STOP	MILES	TOLLS	MISC.

AUTO MILEAGE AND EXPENSE LOG

MONTH:_______________

DATE	PLACE, PERSON OR TASK	START	STOP	MILES	TOLLS	MISC.

AUTO MILEAGE AND EXPENSE LOG

MONTH:_________________

DATE	PLACE, PERSON OR TASK	START	STOP	MILES	TOLLS	MISC.

MONTH:

AUTO MILEAGE AND EXPENSE LOG

MONTH: _______________

DATE	PLACE, PERSON OR TASK	START	STOP	MILES	TOLLS	MISC.

AUTO MILEAGE AND EXPENSE LOG

MONTH:________________

DATE	PLACE, PERSON OR TASK	START	STOP	MILES	TOLLS	MISC.

AUTO MILEAGE AND EXPENSE LOG

MONTH:_______________

DATE	PLACE, PERSON OR TASK	START	STOP	MILES	TOLLS	MISC.

AUTO MILEAGE AND EXPENSE LOG

MONTH: ___________________

DATE	PLACE, PERSON OR TASK	START	STOP	MILES	TOLLS	MISC.

AUTO MILEAGE AND EXPENSE LOG

MONTH:___________________

DATE	PLACE, PERSON OR TASK	START	STOP	MILES	TOLLS	MISC.

AUTO MILEAGE AND EXPENSE LOG

MONTH: _______________

DATE	PLACE, PERSON OR TASK	START	STOP	MILES	TOLLS	MISC.

AUTO MILEAGE AND EXPENSE LOG

MONTH:______________

DATE	PLACE, PERSON OR TASK	START	STOP	MILES	TOLLS	MISC.

AUTO MILEAGE AND EXPENSE LOG

MONTH:_________________

DATE	PLACE, PERSON OR TASK	START	STOP	MILES	TOLLS	MISC.

MONTH:

AUTO MILEAGE AND EXPENSE LOG

MONTH:___________________

DATE	PLACE, PERSON OR TASK	START	STOP	MILES	TOLLS	MISC.

AUTO MILEAGE AND EXPENSE LOG

MONTH: _______________

DATE	PLACE, PERSON OR TASK	START	STOP	MILES	TOLLS	MISC.

AUTO MILEAGE AND EXPENSE LOG

MONTH:_________________

DATE	PLACE, PERSON OR TASK	START	STOP	MILES	TOLLS	MISC.

AUTO MILEAGE AND EXPENSE LOG

MONTH:________________

DATE	PLACE, PERSON OR TASK	START	STOP	MILES	TOLLS	MISC.

AUTO MILEAGE AND EXPENSE LOG

MONTH:________________

DATE	PLACE, PERSON OR TASK	START	STOP	MILES	TOLLS	MISC.

AUTO MILEAGE AND EXPENSE LOG

MONTH:________________

DATE	PLACE, PERSON OR TASK	START	STOP	MILES	TOLLS	MISC.

AUTO MILEAGE AND EXPENSE LOG

MONTH:_________________

DATE	PLACE, PERSON OR TASK	START	STOP	MILES	TOLLS	MISC.

AUTO MILEAGE AND EXPENSE LOG

MONTH:_________________

DATE	PLACE, PERSON OR TASK	START	STOP	MILES	TOLLS	MISC.

AUTO MILEAGE AND EXPENSE LOG

MONTH:_______________

DATE	PLACE, PERSON OR TASK	START	STOP	MILES	TOLLS	MISC.

AUTO MILEAGE AND EXPENSE LOG

MONTH:_________________

DATE	PLACE, PERSON OR TASK	START	STOP	MILES	TOLLS	MISC.

AUTO MILEAGE AND EXPENSE LOG

MONTH:________________

DATE	PLACE, PERSON OR TASK	START	STOP	MILES	TOLLS	MISC.

AUTO MILEAGE AND EXPENSE LOG

MONTH: _______________

DATE	PLACE, PERSON OR TASK	START	STOP	MILES	TOLLS	MISC.

AUTO MILEAGE AND EXPENSE LOG

MONTH:_______________

DATE	PLACE, PERSON OR TASK	START	STOP	MILES	TOLLS	MISC.

AUTO MILEAGE AND EXPENSE LOG

MONTH: _______________

DATE	PLACE, PERSON OR TASK	START	STOP	MILES	TOLLS	MISC.

AUTO MILEAGE AND EXPENSE LOG

MONTH: _______________

DATE	PLACE, PERSON OR TASK	START	STOP	MILES	TOLLS	MISC.

AUTO MILEAGE AND EXPENSE LOG

MONTH:_______________

DATE	PLACE, PERSON OR TASK	START	STOP	MILES	TOLLS	MISC.

MONTH:_______________

AUTO MILEAGE AND EXPENSE LOG

MONTH:_________________

DATE	PLACE, PERSON OR TASK	START	STOP	MILES	TOLLS	MISC.

AUTO MILEAGE AND EXPENSE LOG

MONTH:_______________

DATE	PLACE, PERSON OR TASK	START	STOP	MILES	TOLLS	MISC.

AUTO MILEAGE AND EXPENSE LOG

MONTH: ________________

DATE	PLACE, PERSON OR TASK	START	STOP	MILES	TOLLS	MISC.

AUTO MILEAGE AND EXPENSE LOG

MONTH: _______________

DATE	PLACE, PERSON OR TASK	START	STOP	MILES	TOLLS	MISC.

AUTO MILEAGE AND EXPENSE LOG

MONTH:_______________

DATE	PLACE, PERSON OR TASK	START	STOP	MILES	TOLLS	MISC.

AUTO MILEAGE AND EXPENSE LOG

MONTH:________________

DATE	PLACE, PERSON OR TASK	START	STOP	MILES	TOLLS	MISC.

AUTO MILEAGE AND EXPENSE LOG

MONTH:_________________

DATE	PLACE, PERSON OR TASK	START	STOP	MILES	TOLLS	MISC.

AUTO MILEAGE AND EXPENSE LOG

MONTH:________________

DATE	PLACE, PERSON OR TASK	START	STOP	MILES	TOLLS	MISC.

AUTO MILEAGE AND EXPENSE LOG

MONTH: _________________

DATE	PLACE, PERSON OR TASK	START	STOP	MILES	TOLLS	MISC.

AUTO MILEAGE AND EXPENSE LOG

MONTH:________________

DATE	PLACE, PERSON OR TASK	START	STOP	MILES	TOLLS	MISC.

AUTO MILEAGE AND EXPENSE LOG

MONTH: _______________

DATE	PLACE, PERSON OR TASK	START	STOP	MILES	TOLLS	MISC.

AUTO MILEAGE AND EXPENSE LOG

MONTH:________________

DATE	PLACE, PERSON OR TASK	START	STOP	MILES	TOLLS	MISC.

AUTO MILEAGE AND EXPENSE LOG

MONTH:_______________

DATE	PLACE, PERSON OR TASK	START	STOP	MILES	TOLLS	MISC.

AUTO MILEAGE AND EXPENSE LOG

MONTH: _________________

DATE	PLACE, PERSON OR TASK	START	STOP	MILES	TOLLS	MISC.

AUTO MILEAGE AND EXPENSE LOG

MONTH: _______________

DATE	PLACE, PERSON OR TASK	START	STOP	MILES	TOLLS	MISC.

AUTO MILEAGE AND EXPENSE LOG

MONTH:________________

DATE	PLACE, PERSON OR TASK	START	STOP	MILES	TOLLS	MISC.

MONTH:________________

AUTO MILEAGE AND EXPENSE LOG

MONTH:________________

DATE	PLACE, PERSON OR TASK	START	STOP	MILES	TOLLS	MISC.

AUTO MILEAGE AND EXPENSE LOG

MONTH: ___________________

DATE	PLACE, PERSON OR TASK	START	STOP	MILES	TOLLS	MISC.

MONTH:

AUTO MILEAGE AND EXPENSE LOG

MONTH: ______________

DATE	PLACE, PERSON OR TASK	START	STOP	MILES	TOLLS	MISC.

MONTH: ______________

AUTO MILEAGE AND EXPENSE LOG

MONTH:_______________

DATE	PLACE, PERSON OR TASK	START	STOP	MILES	TOLLS	MISC.

AUTO MILEAGE AND EXPENSE LOG

MONTH:_______________

DATE	PLACE, PERSON OR TASK	START	STOP	MILES	TOLLS	MISC.

AUTO MILEAGE AND EXPENSE LOG

MONTH:________________

DATE	PLACE, PERSON OR TASK	START	STOP	MILES	TOLLS	MISC.

MONTH:________________

AUTO MILEAGE AND EXPENSE LOG

MONTH: _______________

DATE	PLACE, PERSON OR TASK	START	STOP	MILES	TOLLS	MISC.

AUTO MILEAGE AND EXPENSE LOG

MONTH:_______________

DATE	PLACE, PERSON OR TASK	START	STOP	MILES	TOLLS	MISC.

AUTO MILEAGE AND EXPENSE LOG

MONTH:_________________

DATE	PLACE, PERSON OR TASK	START	STOP	MILES	TOLLS	MISC.

AUTO MILEAGE AND EXPENSE LOG

MONTH:________________

DATE	PLACE, PERSON OR TASK	START	STOP	MILES	TOLLS	MISC.

AUTO MILEAGE AND EXPENSE LOG

MONTH:________________

DATE	PLACE, PERSON OR TASK	START	STOP	MILES	TOLLS	MISC.

AUTO MILEAGE AND EXPENSE LOG

MONTH:_______________

DATE	PLACE, PERSON OR TASK	START	STOP	MILES	TOLLS	MISC.

AUTO MILEAGE AND EXPENSE LOG

MONTH: ___________________

DATE	PLACE, PERSON OR TASK	START	STOP	MILES	TOLLS	MISC.

AUTO MILEAGE AND EXPENSE LOG

MONTH:_______________

DATE	PLACE, PERSON OR TASK	START	STOP	MILES	TOLLS	MISC.

AUTO MILEAGE AND EXPENSE LOG

MONTH:_______________

DATE	PLACE, PERSON OR TASK	START	STOP	MILES	TOLLS	MISC.

AUTO MILEAGE AND EXPENSE LOG

MONTH:_______________

DATE	PLACE, PERSON OR TASK	START	STOP	MILES	TOLLS	MISC.

AUTO MILEAGE AND EXPENSE LOG

MONTH:_________________

DATE	PLACE, PERSON OR TASK	START	STOP	MILES	TOLLS	MISC.

AUTO MILEAGE AND EXPENSE LOG

MONTH: ___________________

DATE	PLACE, PERSON OR TASK	START	STOP	MILES	TOLLS	MISC.

MONTH: ___________________

AUTO MILEAGE AND EXPENSE LOG

MONTH:_________________

DATE	PLACE, PERSON OR TASK	START	STOP	MILES	TOLLS	MISC.

AUTO MILEAGE AND EXPENSE LOG

MONTH: ________________

DATE	PLACE, PERSON OR TASK	START	STOP	MILES	TOLLS	MISC.

AUTO MILEAGE AND EXPENSE LOG

MONTH:_________________

DATE	PLACE, PERSON OR TASK	START	STOP	MILES	TOLLS	MISC.

AUTO MILEAGE AND EXPENSE LOG

MONTH:________________

DATE	PLACE, PERSON OR TASK	START	STOP	MILES	TOLLS	MISC.
MONTH:						

AUTO MILEAGE AND EXPENSE LOG

MONTH:_______________

DATE	PLACE, PERSON OR TASK	START	STOP	MILES	TOLLS	MISC.

AUTO MILEAGE AND EXPENSE LOG

MONTH:_______________

DATE	PLACE, PERSON OR TASK	START	STOP	MILES	TOLLS	MISC.

AUTO MILEAGE AND EXPENSE LOG

MONTH:_______________

DATE	PLACE, PERSON OR TASK	START	STOP	MILES	TOLLS	MISC.